RADIOHEAD KID A

W.A.S.T.E. LETTERS:
P.O. BOX 322, OXFORD, OX4 1EY, UK
RADIOHEAD.COM IS FOR USE WITH A COMPUTER

PRODUCTION OF MUSIC BOOK BY: ANNA JOYCE
MUSIC ARRANGED AND ENGRAVED BY: ARTEMIS MUSIC LTD
LANDSCAPES, KNIVES AND GLUE: STANLEY AND TCHOCK

EVERYTHING IN ITS RIGHT PLACE

**Words and Music by Thomas Yorke, Philip Selway,
Edward O'Brien, Colin Greenwood and Jonathan Greenwood**

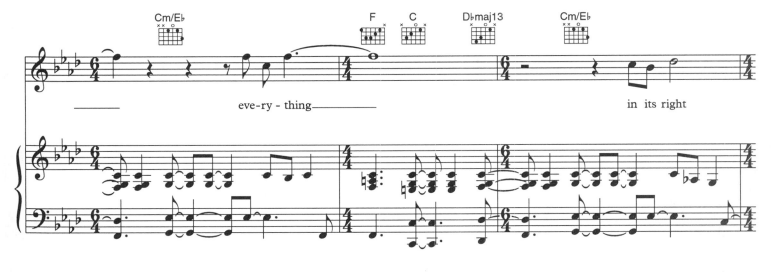

eve-ry - thing _____ in its right

place, _____ in its right place, _____

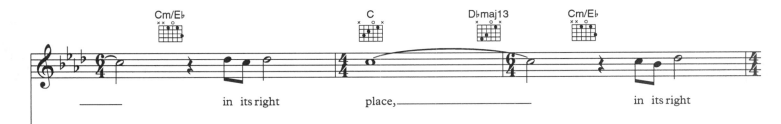

_____ in its right place, _____ in its right

Verse

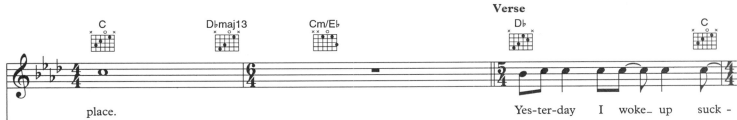

place. Yes-ter-day I woke_ up suck-

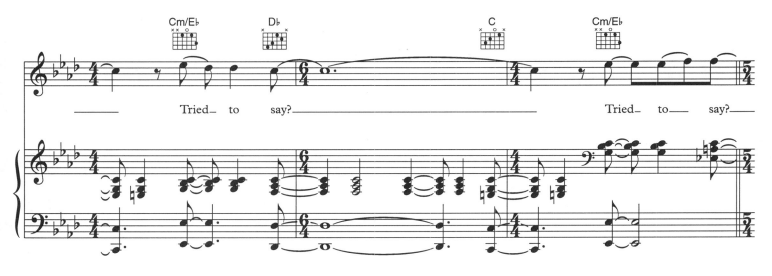

Tried to say?   Tried to say?

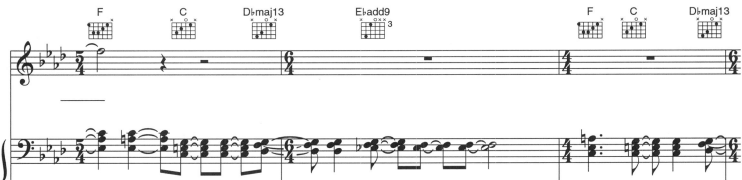

Bridge

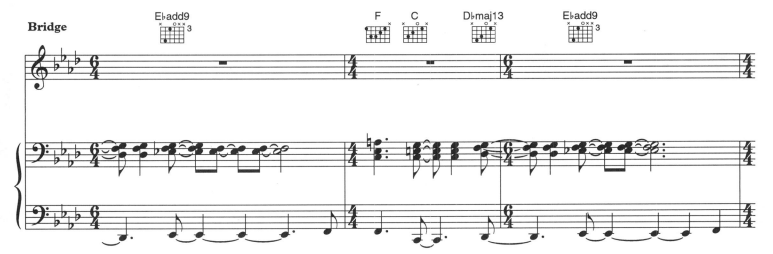

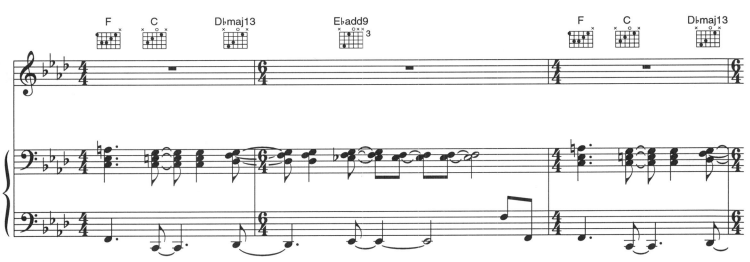

7

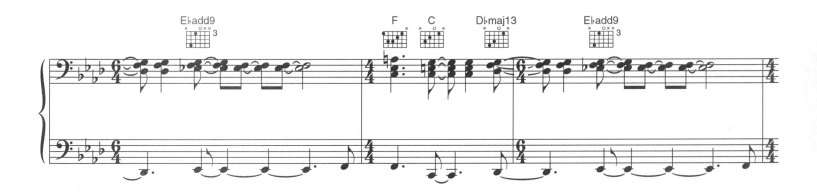

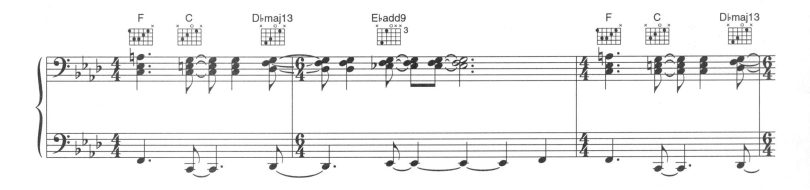

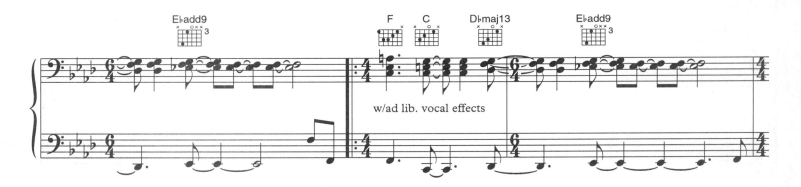

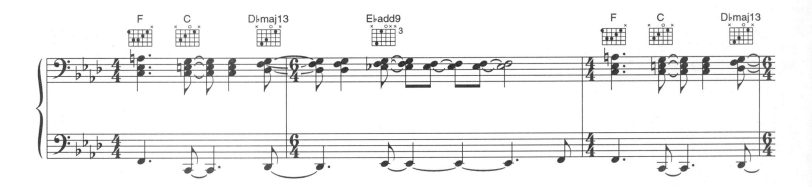

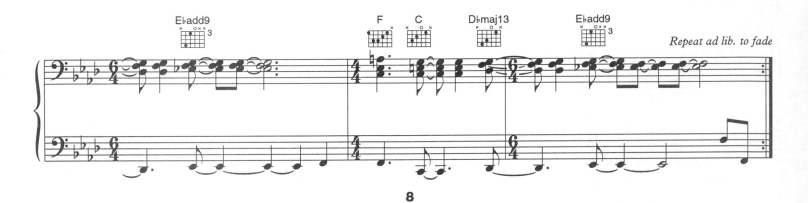

KID A

**Words and Music by Thomas Yorke, Philip Selway,
Edward O'Brien, Colin Greenwood and Jonathan Greenwood**

I slipped on a lit - tle white__ lie.

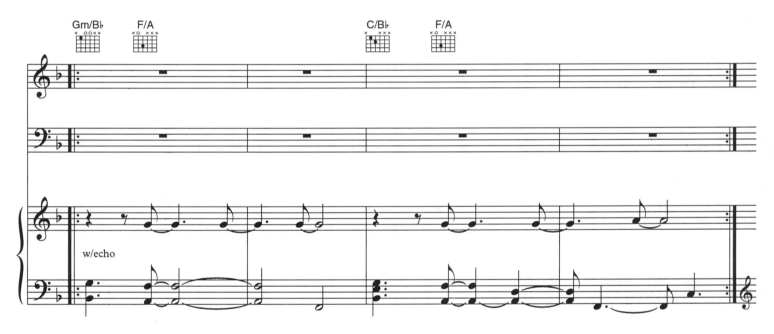

w/echo

Verse

We've got__ heads__ on sticks   and

tacet 1°

Bridge

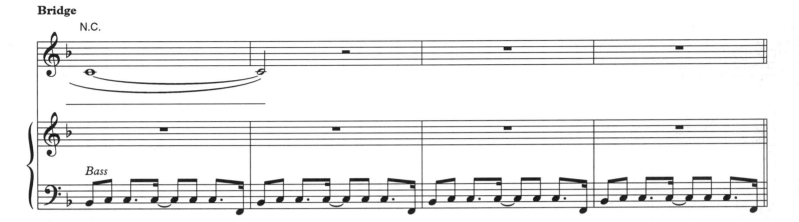

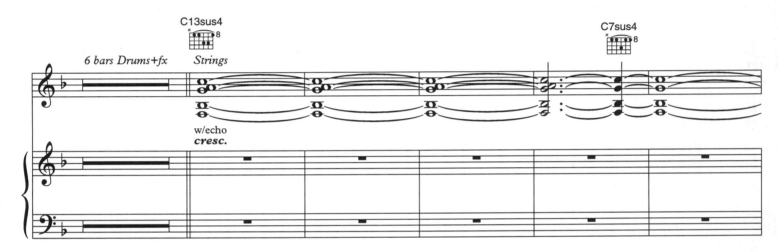

Verse

C13sus4

rats   and the child - ren will   fol - low me out___ of   town.___

The

13

Rats and child-ren___ fol-low me out___ of town.___ C'mon kids!

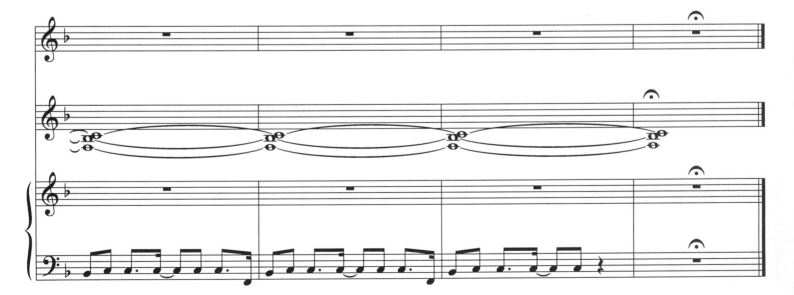

THE NATIONAL ANTHEM

Words and Music by Thomas Yorke, Philip Selway,
Edward O'Brien, Colin Greenwood and Jonathan Greenwood

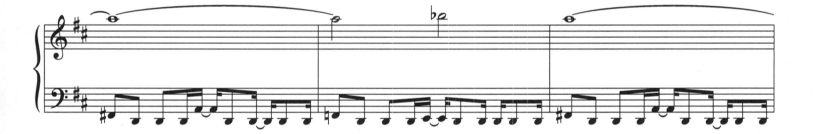

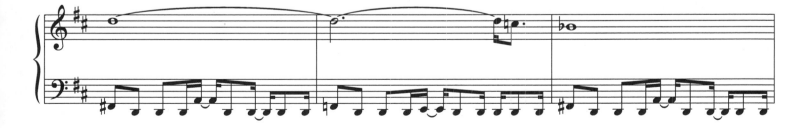

Verse

1. Eve-ry - one,— eve-ry - one— a - round— here.
2. Eve-ry - one,— eve-ry - one— is so— near.

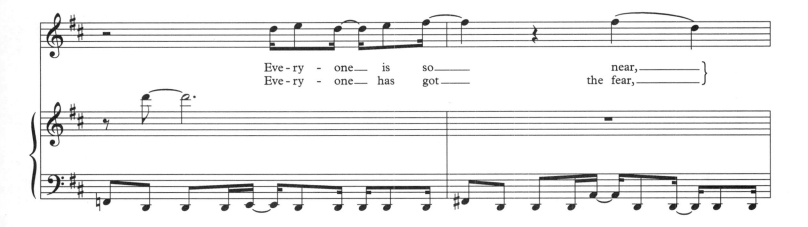

Eve-ry - one— is so— near,——
Eve-ry - one— has got— the fear,——

hol - ding on,— it's hol - ding on.—

1° vocal tacet

It's hol - ding on._____

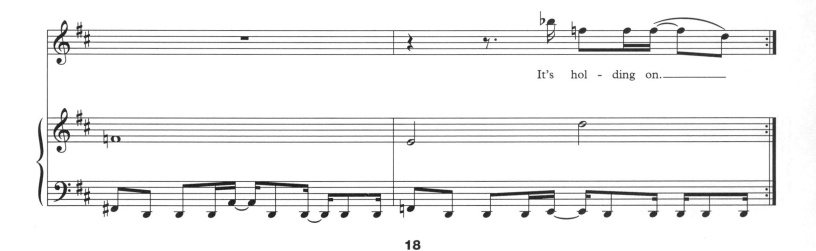

It's hol - ding on._____

18

HOW TO DISAPPEAR COMPLETELY

Words and Music by Thomas Yorke, Philip Selway, Edward O'Brien, Colin Greenwood and Jonathan Greenwood

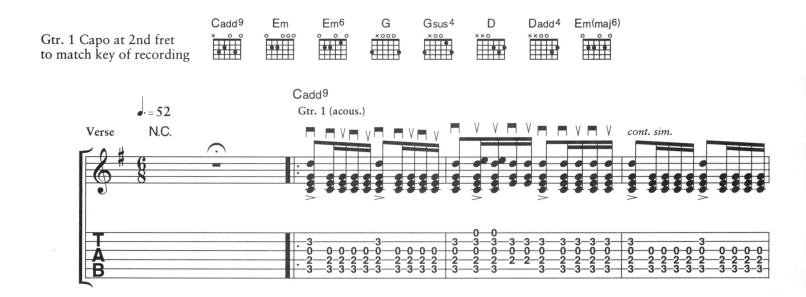

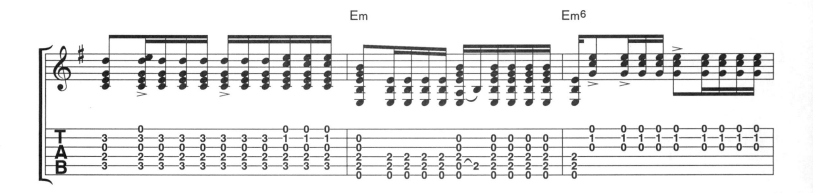

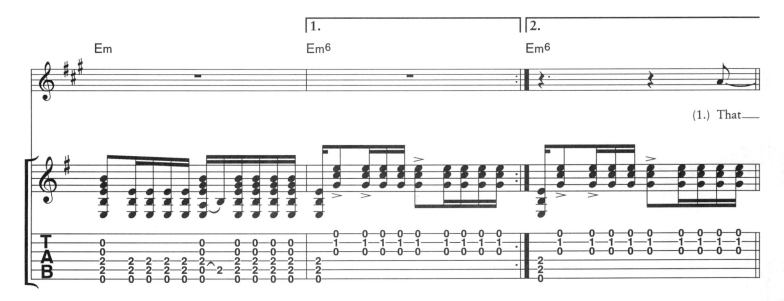

Verse

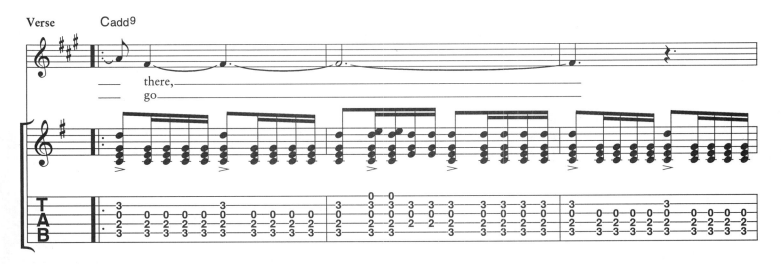

there,
go

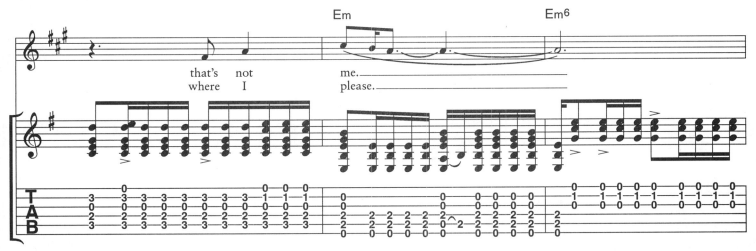

that's not me.
where I please.

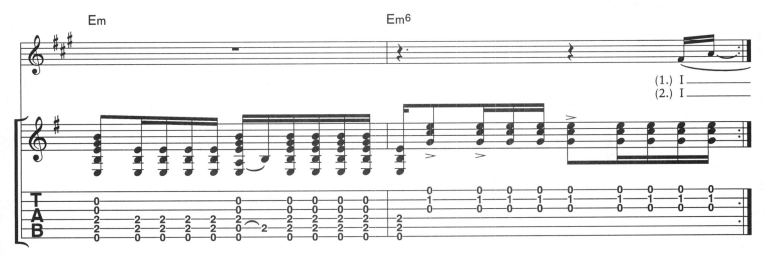

(1.) I
(2.) I

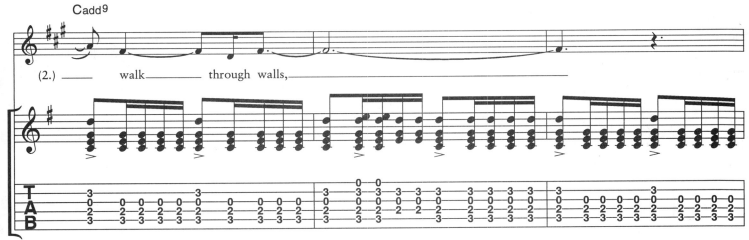

(2.) walk through walls,

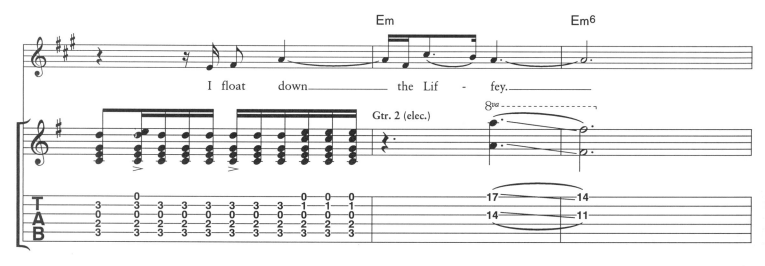

I float down_____ the Lif - fey._____

Gtr. 2 (elec.)

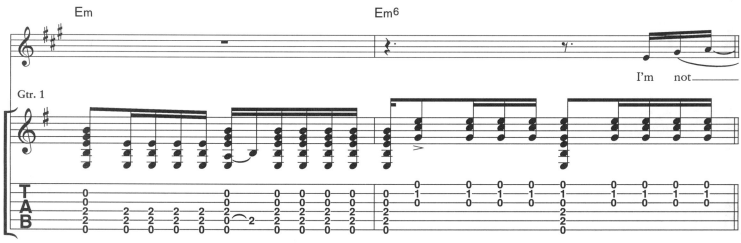

Gtr. 1

I'm not_____

Chorus 𝄋 G

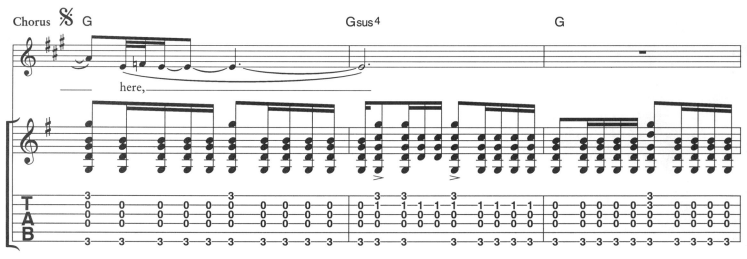

_____ here,_____

this is - n't_____ hap - pen - ing._____

Gsus⁴

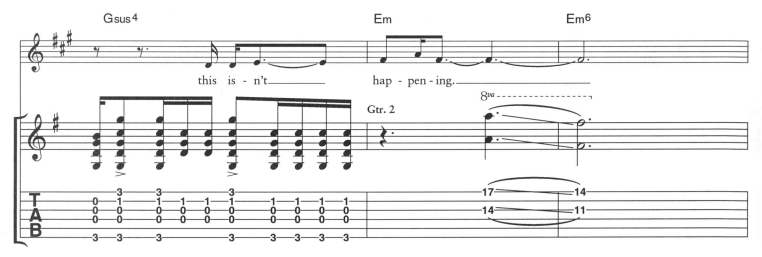

Gtr. 2

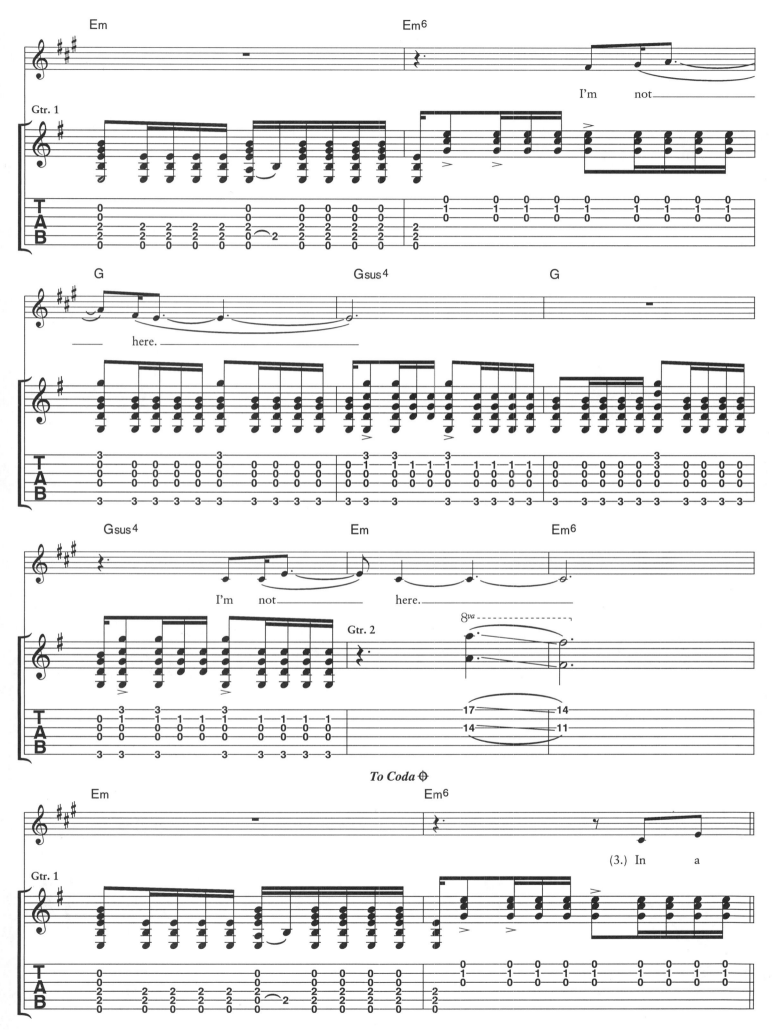

Verse

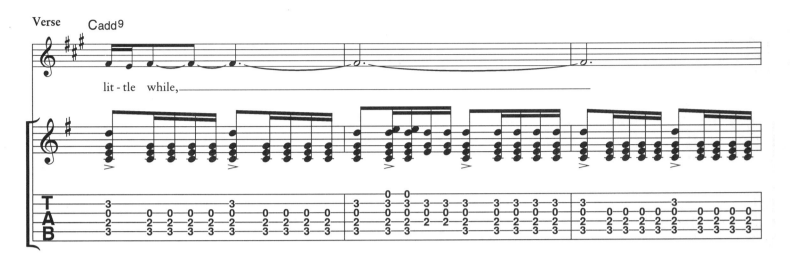

lit - tle while,

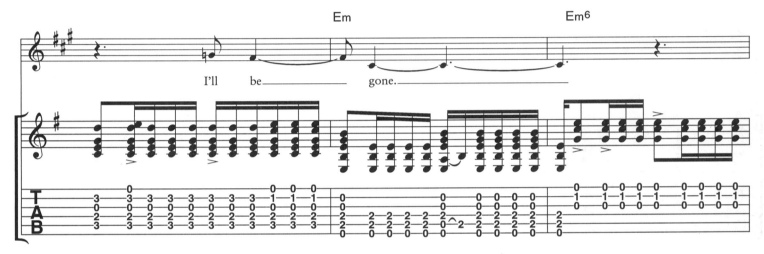

I'll be gone.

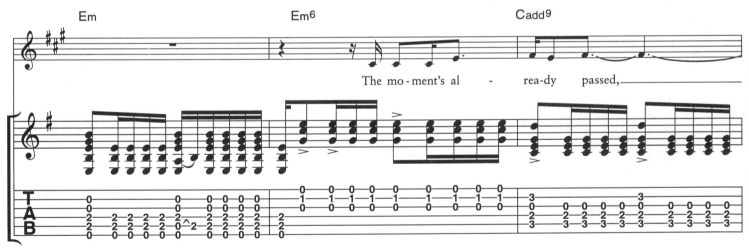

The mo - ment's al - rea-dy passed,

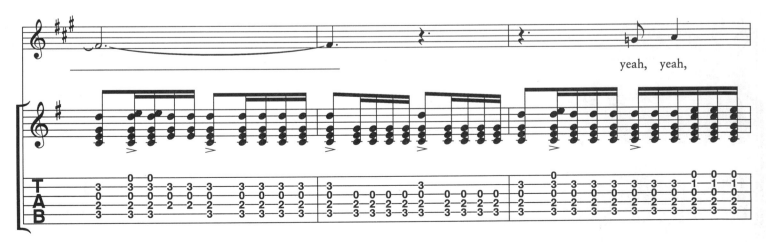

yeah, yeah,

24

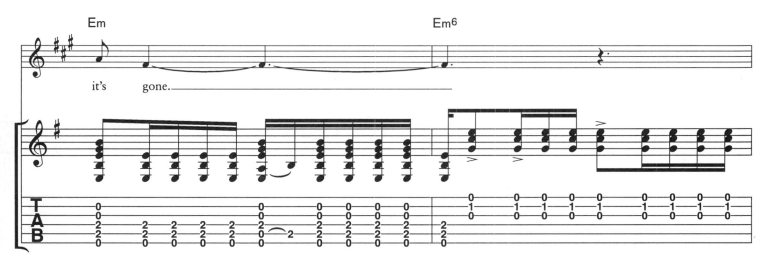

it's gone._____

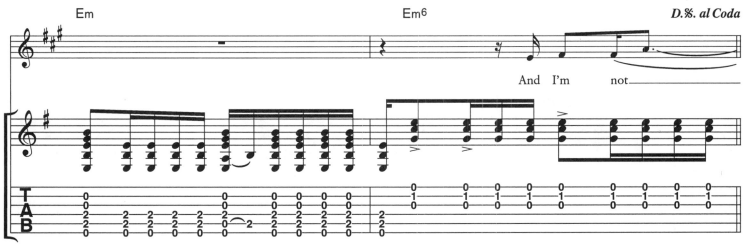

D.%. al Coda

And I'm not_____

Ⓒ *Coda*

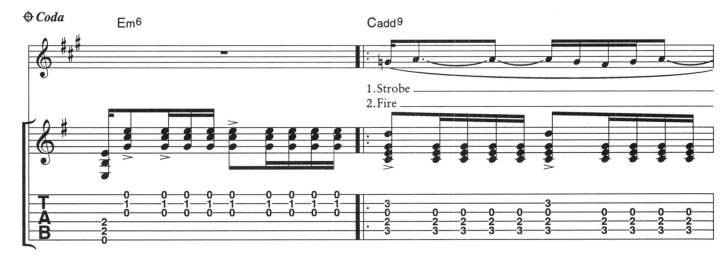

1.Strobe _____
2.Fire _____

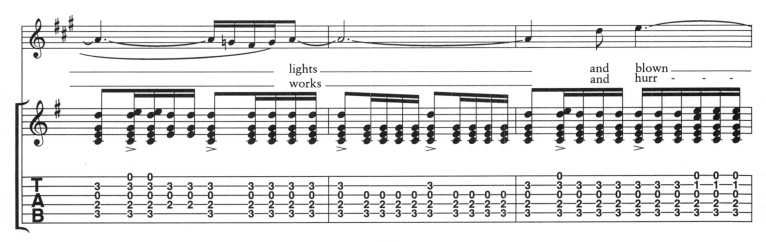

lights _____
works

and blown _____
and hurr - -

25

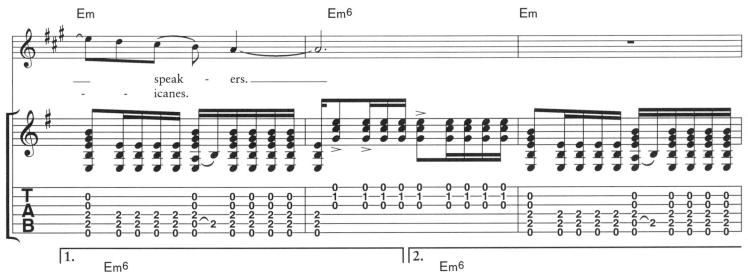

speak - ers.

- - icanes.

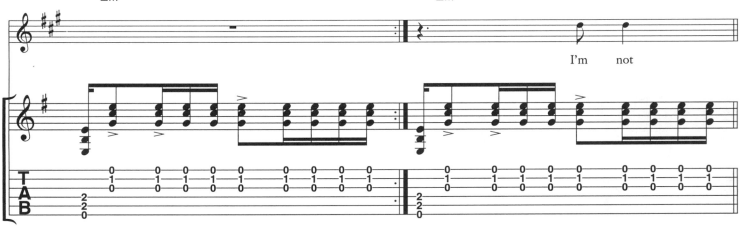

1.

2.

I'm not

Chorus

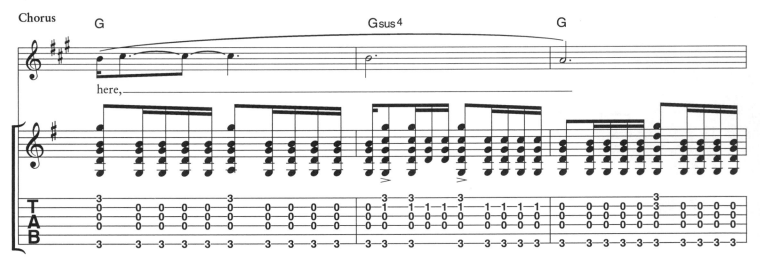

here,

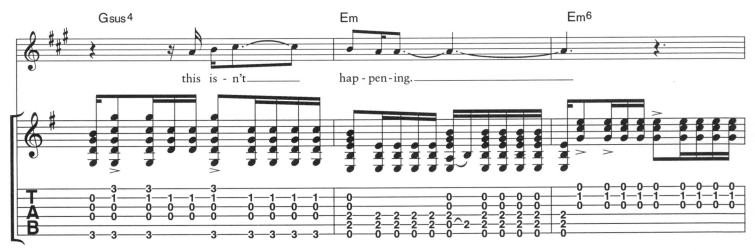

this is - n't hap - pen - ing.

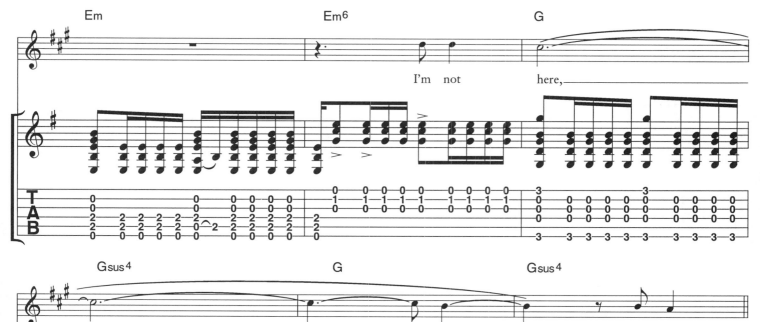

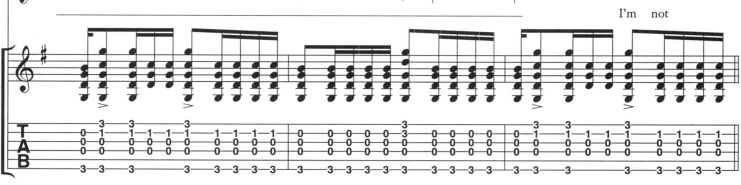

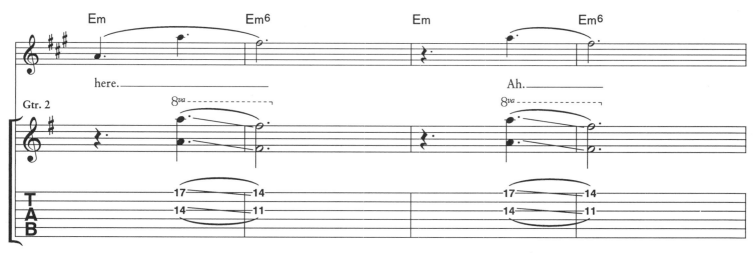

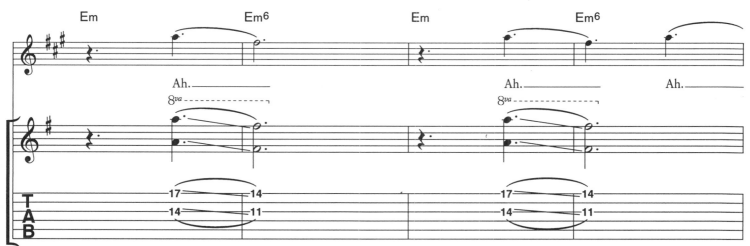

27

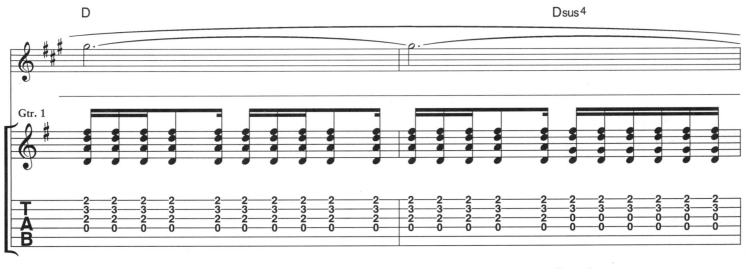

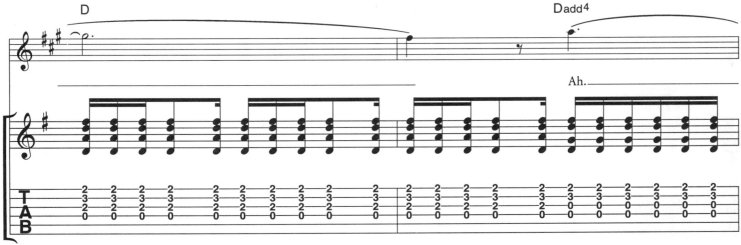

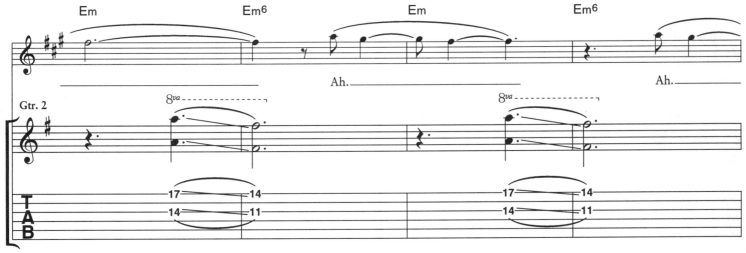

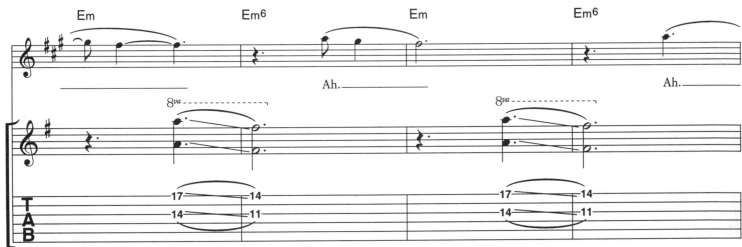

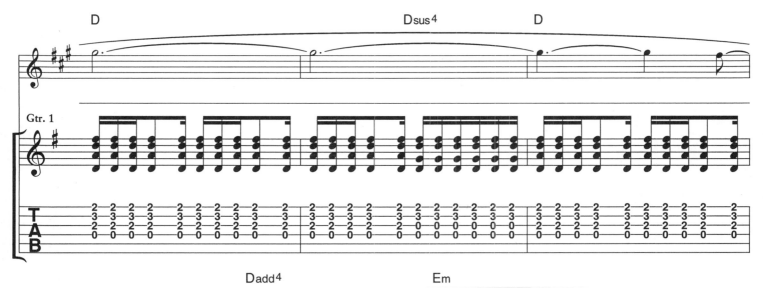

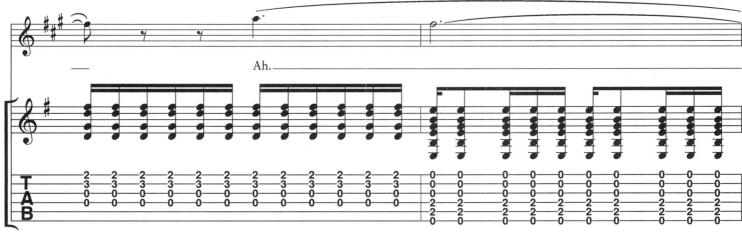

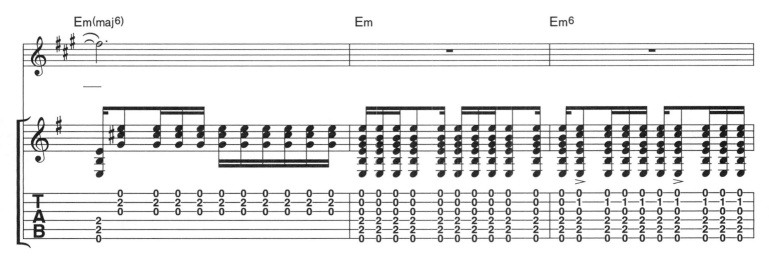

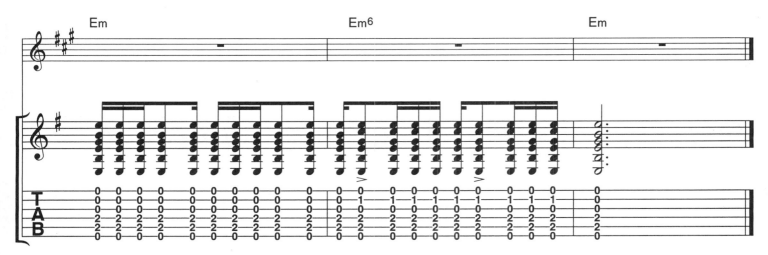

TREEFINGERS

Music by Thomas Yorke, Philip Selway, Edward O'Brien, Colin Greenwood and Jonathan Greenwood

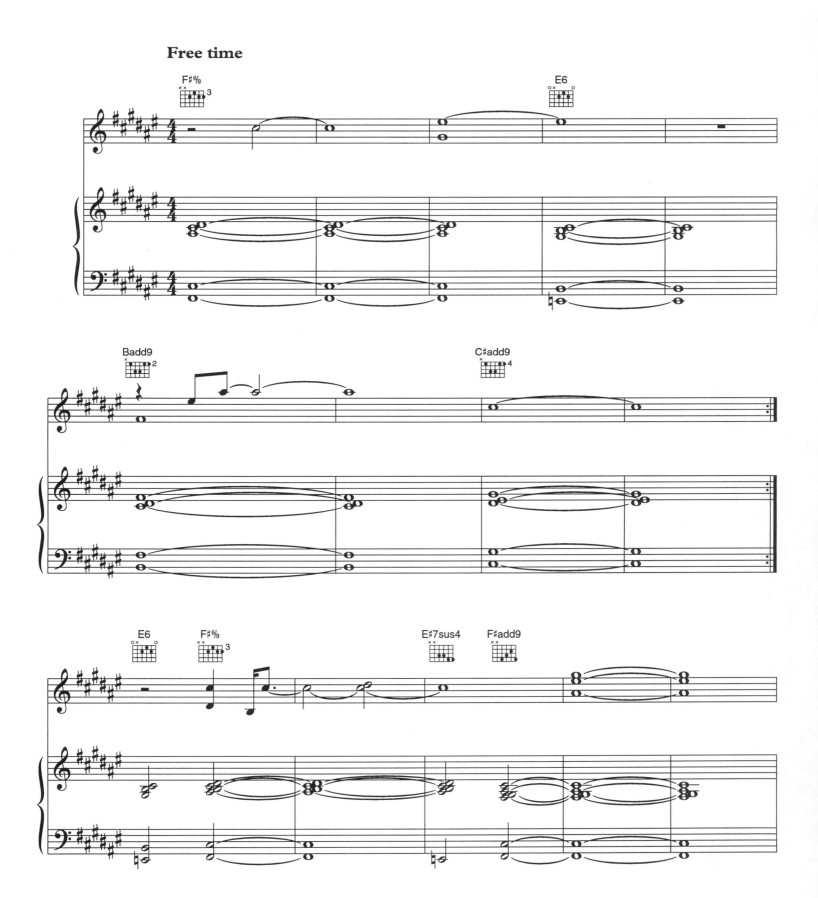

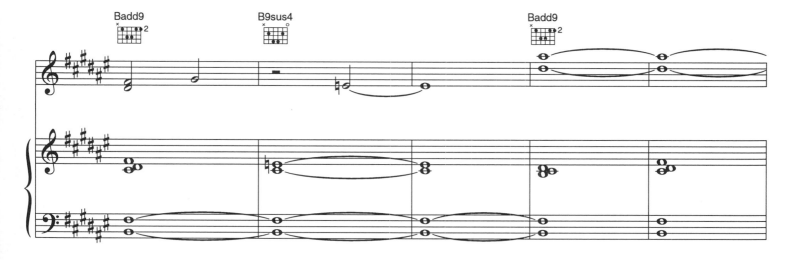

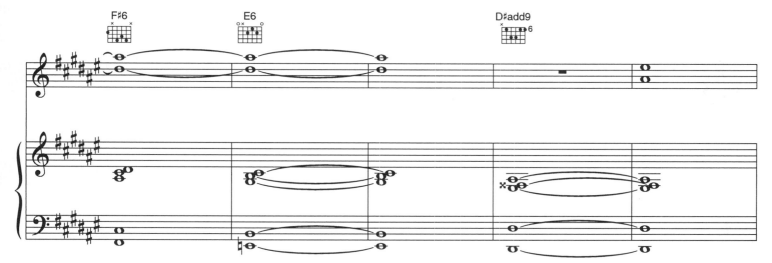

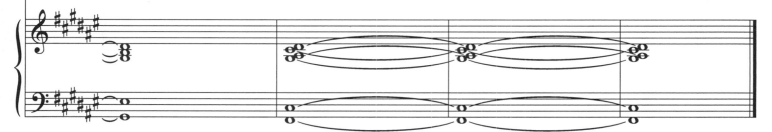

OPTIMISTIC

**Words and Music by Thomas Yorke, Philip Selway,
Edward O'Brien, Colin Greenwood and Jonathan Greenwood**

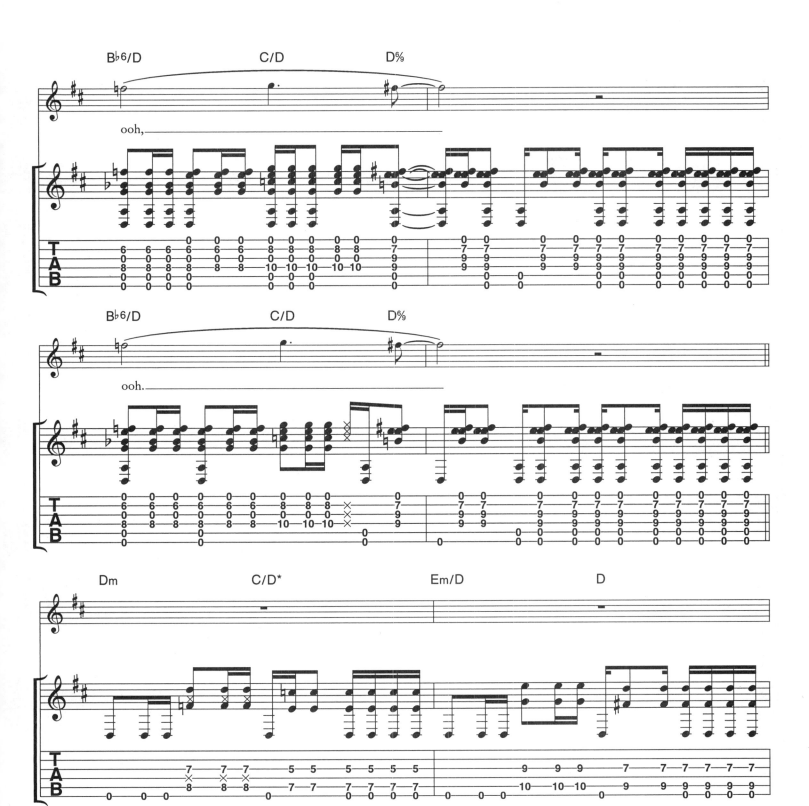

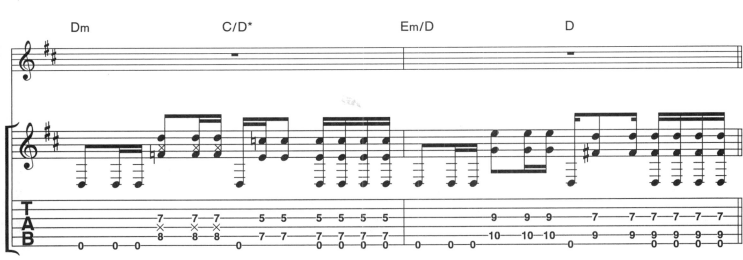

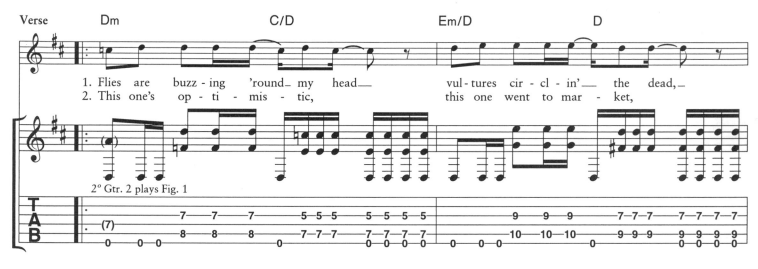

1. Flies are buzz-ing 'round my head___ vul-tures cir-cl-in'___ the dead,___
2. This one's op-ti-mis-tic, this one went to mar-ket,

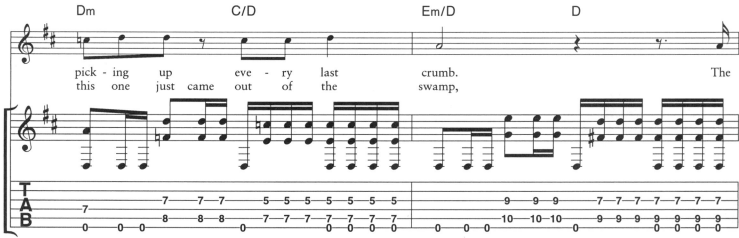

pick-ing up eve-ry last crumb. The
this one just came out of the swamp,

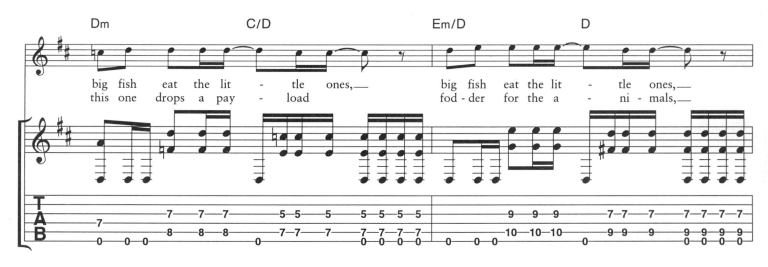

big fish eat the lit-tle ones,___ big fish eat the lit-tle ones,___
this one drops a pay-load fod-der for the a-ni-mals,___

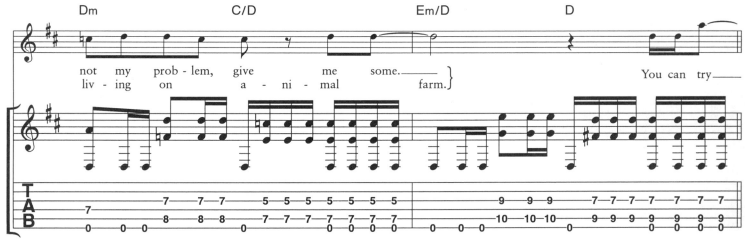

not my prob-lem, give me some.___ You can try___
liv-ing on a-ni-mal farm.}

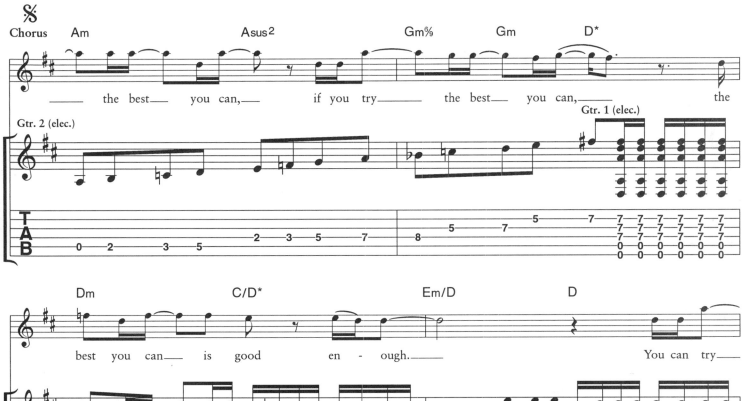

Chorus

the best you can, if you try the best you can, the

best you can is good en - ough. You can try

the best you can, if you try the best you can, the

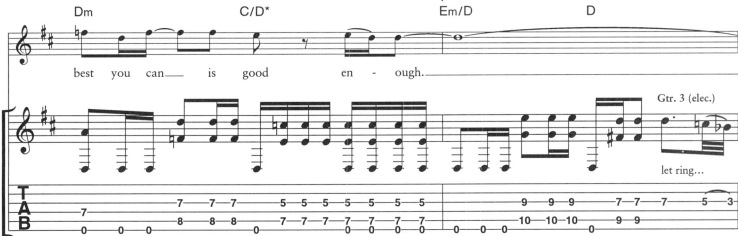

best you can is good en - ough.

let ring...

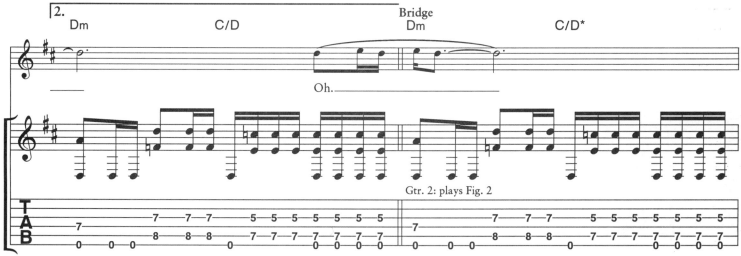

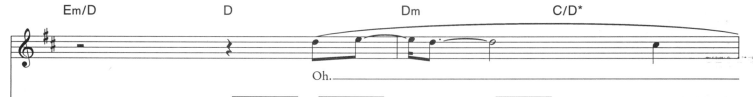

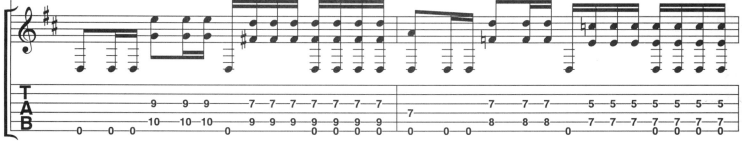

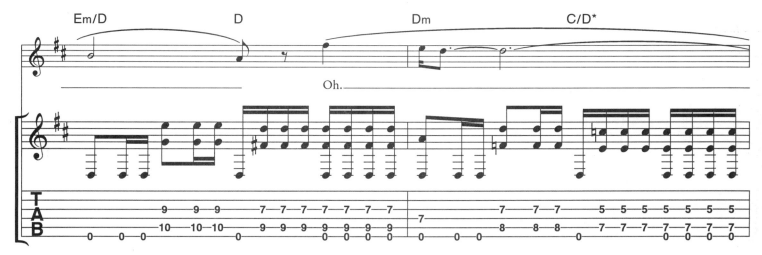

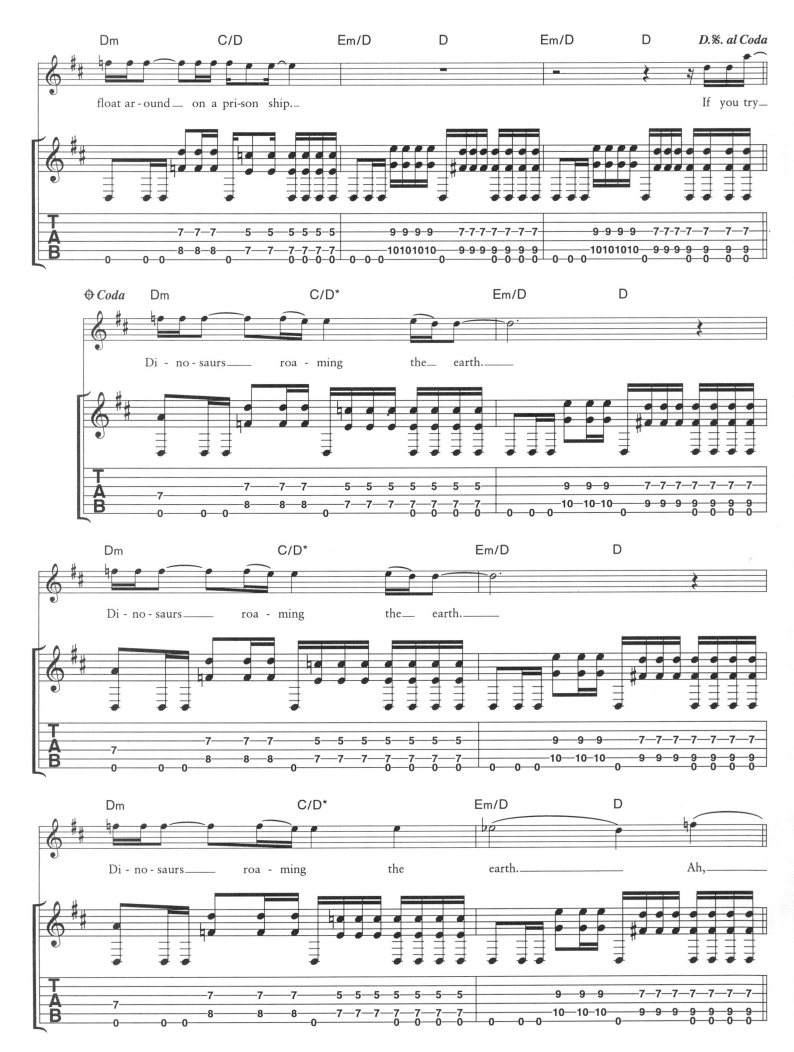

38

IN LIMBO

**Words and Music by Thomas Yorke, Philip Selway,
Edward O'Brien, Colin Greenwood and Jonathan Greenwood**

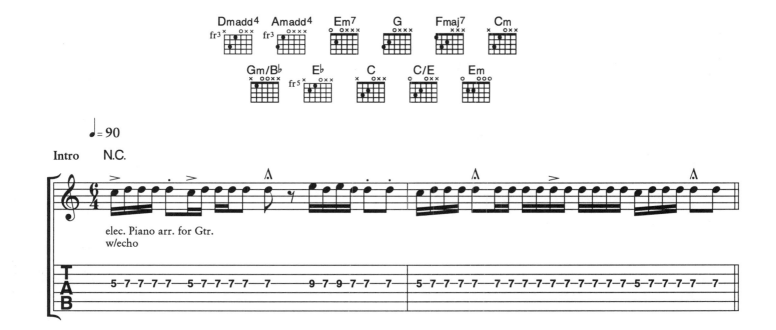

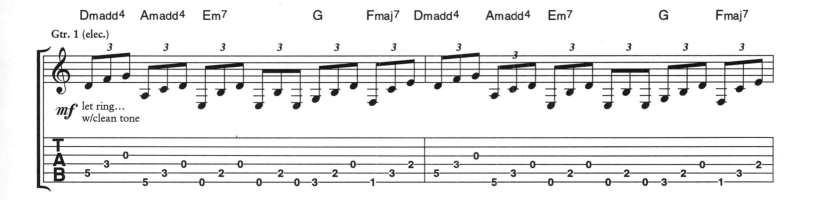

IDIOTEQUE

Words and Music by Thomas Yorke, Philip Selway, Edward O'Brien, Colin Greenwood, Jonathan Greenwood and Paul Lansky

Here ____ I'm all-owed, ____ ev-'ry-thing all ____ of the time. ____

49

MORNING BELL

**Words and Music by Thomas Yorke, Philip Selway,
Edward O'Brien, Colin Greenwood and Jonathan Greenwood**

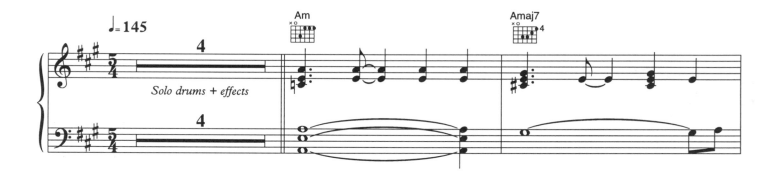

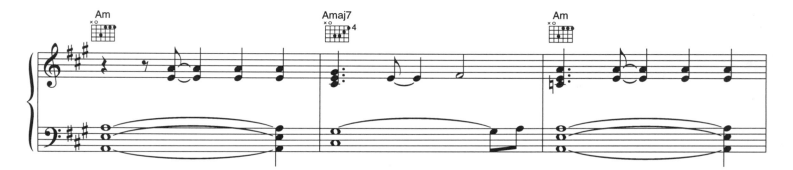

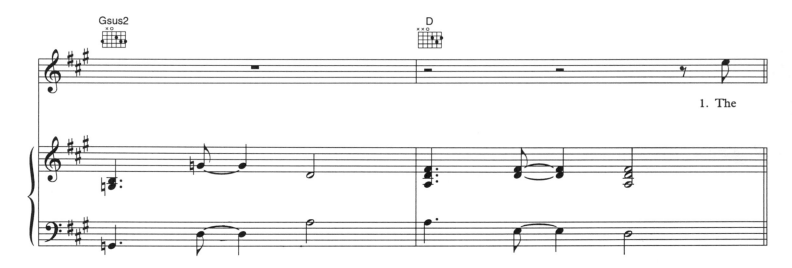

Verse

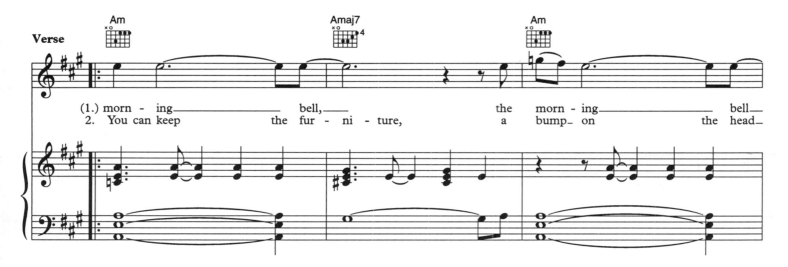

(1.) morn - ing_____ bell,_____ the morn - ing_____ bell_____
2. You can keep the fur - ni - ture, a bump_ on the head_

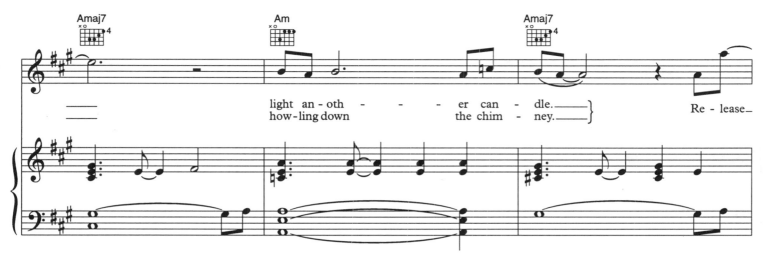

light an - oth - - - er can - dle._____ Re - lease_
how - ling down the chim - ney._____ }

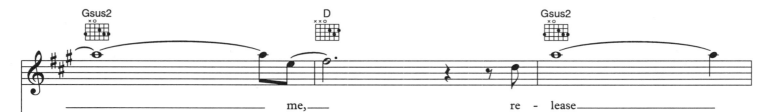

_____ me,_____ re - lease_____

me. Please_____

51

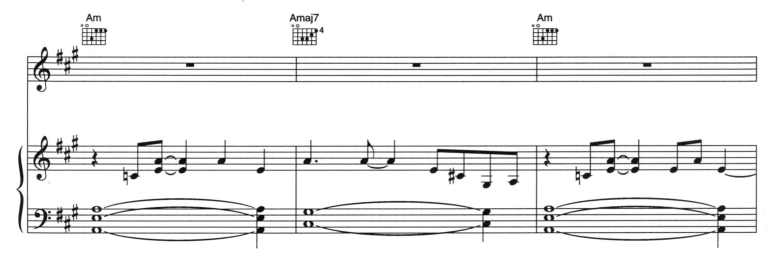

re - lease _____ me, ____ re -

- lease _____ me. Where'd you park the car? ____

Where'd you park _____ the car? ____

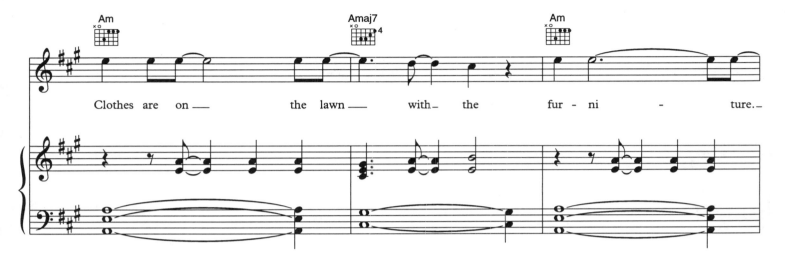

Clothes are on —— the lawn —— with— the fur - ni - ture.—

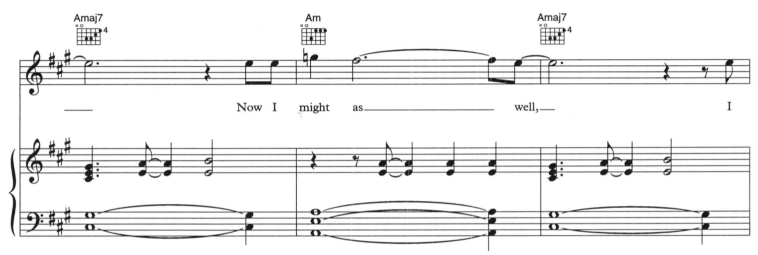

—— Now I might as—————— well,—— I

might as————— well,— slee-py jack the fire——— drill.

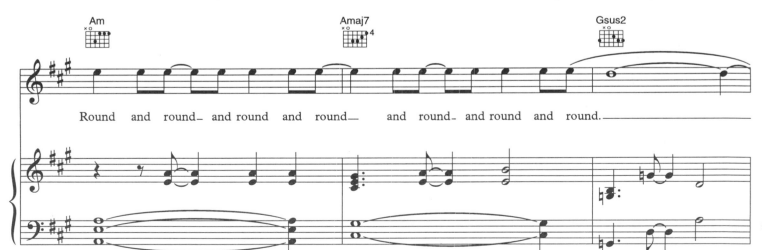

Round and round— and round and round—— and round— and round and round.————

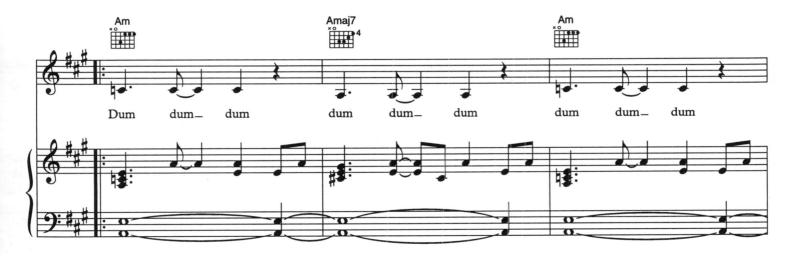

Dum dum— dum   dum dum— dum   dum dum— dum

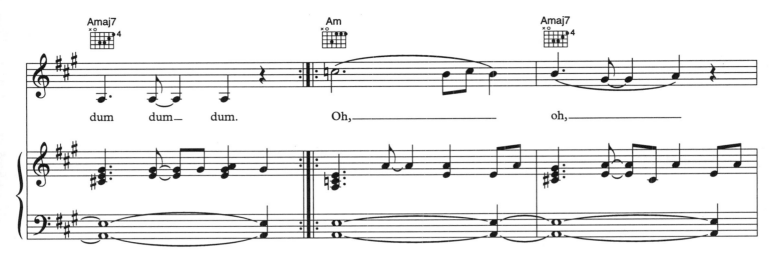

dum dum— dum.   Oh,_____   oh,_____

oh,_____   oh,_____   oh,_____

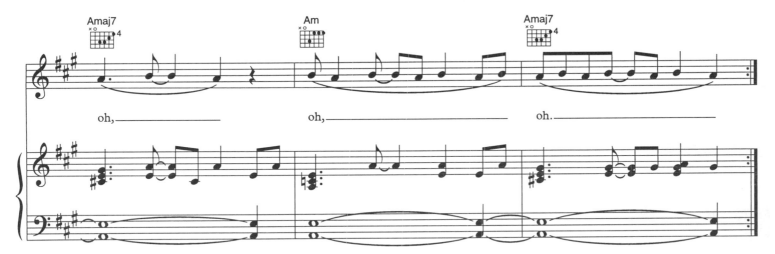

oh,_____   oh,_____   oh.

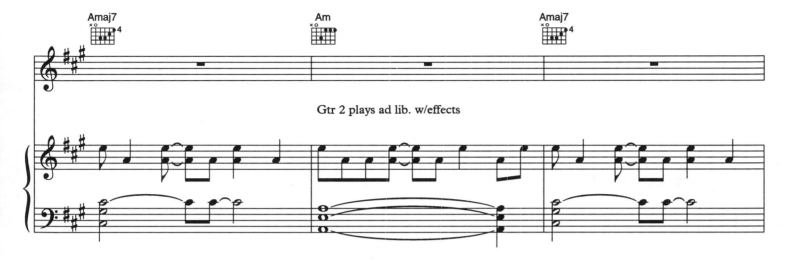

Gtr 2 plays ad lib. w/effects

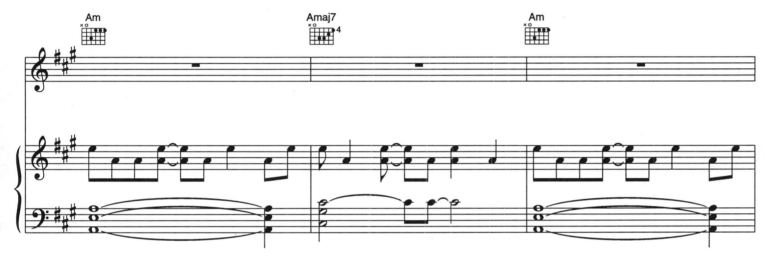

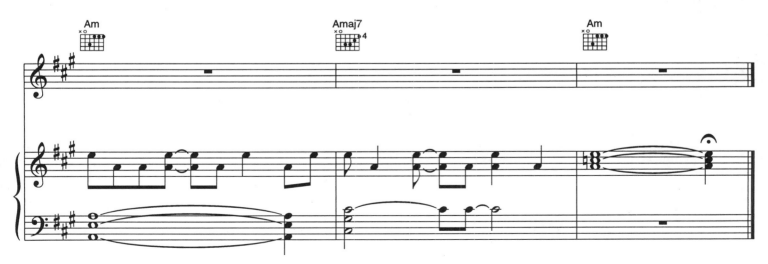

MOTION PICTURE SOUNDTRACK

**Words and Music by Thomas Yorke, Philip Selway,
Edward O'Brien, Colin Greenwood and Jonathan Greenwood**

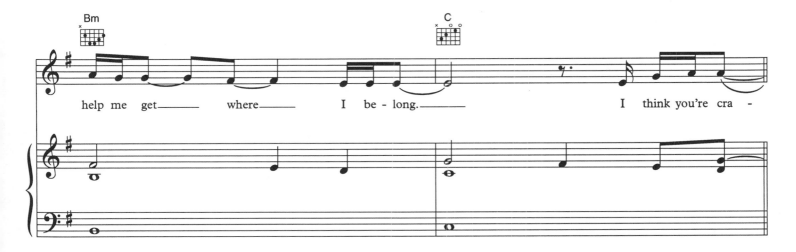

help me get_____ where_____ I be - long._____ I think you're cra -

Chorus

- - - zy, may - - - be. I think you're cra - - - - zy

rall.   **Verse**

may - - be. Stop send - ing let - - ters,___

let - ters___ al - ways___ get burned.___ It's not like the

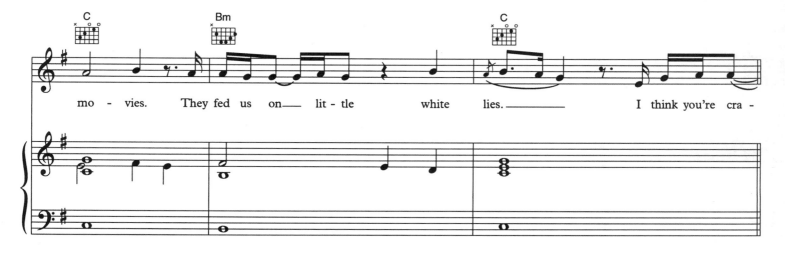

mo - vies. They fed us on— lit - tle white lies.———— I think you're cra -

Chorus

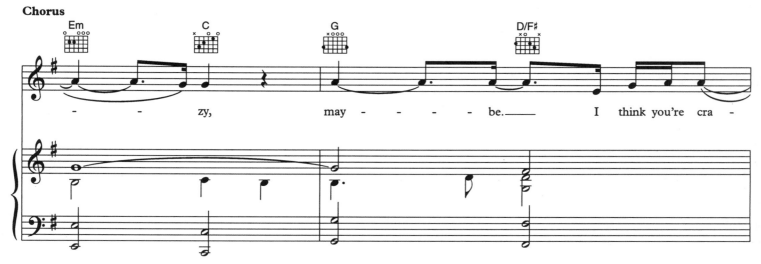

- - zy, may - - - be.—— I think you're cra -

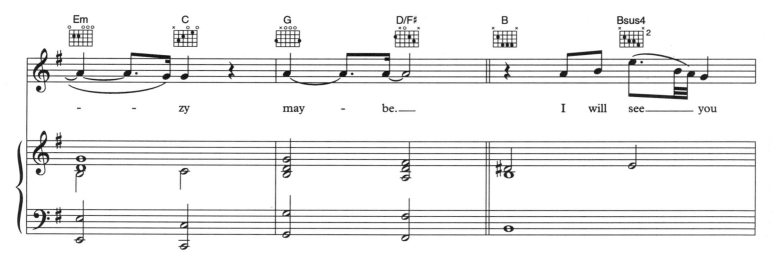

- - zy may - be.—— I will see—— you

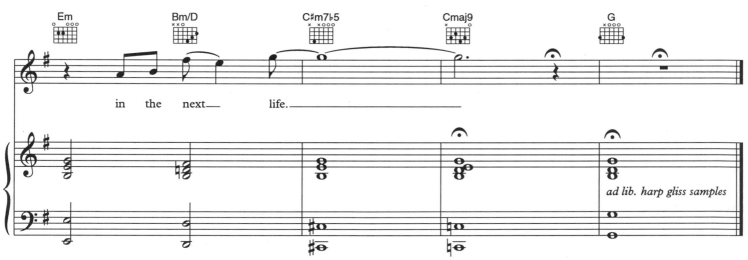

in the next— life.———————————

ad lib. harp gliss samples